80 6042888 1
WITHDRAWN FROM ST
D0335130

Best Poems of 1956

BEST POEMS of 1956

BORESTONE MOUNTAIN POETRY AWARDS 1957

A Compilation of Original Poetry published in Magazines of the English-speaking World in 1956

Ninth Annual Issue

STANFORD UNIVERSITY PRESS • STANFORD, CALIFORNIA
1957

ANNOUNCEMENT OF AWARDS, AND ACKNOWLEDGMENTS

The poems in this our ninth annual compilation of magazine poetry of the English-speaking world were selected by our 1957 Editorial Board from poetry published during the year 1956. The advisory editors were Lionel Stevenson (chairman), Hildegarde Flanner, Frances Minturn Howard, Gertrude Claytor, and Howard Sergeant (who has covered the poetry of the British Commonwealth with the exception of Canada). Prizes have been awarded to three poets for poems chosen by the editors for first, second, and third place in our contest; the winning poems are indicated in the Table of Contents.

The editors gratefully acknowledge permission to reprint the poems listed on the Contents pages from the magazines, publishers, and authors owning the copyrights. Poems requiring special forms of citation are listed below.

ROBERT T. MOORE, *Editor in Chief*
Borestone Mountain Poetry Awards

"The Song" (p. 3), by W. H. Auden, is reprinted with the permission of the author. "The Child Hermes" (p. 4) is reprinted with the permission of *The Lyric* and with the permission of the author's American publisher, J. B. Lippincott Company, from *A Letter to Lucian and Other Poems* by Alfred Noyes. "The Wall of Rome" (p. 16) is reprinted with the permission of *The Yale Review*, copyright 1956 by Yale University Press. "Sparrow in the House" (p. 38) is reprinted from *Prairie Schooner* with the permission of the University of Nebraska Press. "We Gathered in the Yard" (p. 50) is reprinted by special permission of *The Saturday Evening Post*, copyright © 1956 by The Curtis Publishing Company. "A Letter for Allhallows" (p. 30), "Jesu, Joy of Man's Desiring" (p. 33), "Carry Me Back" (p. 42), "Iceberg" (p. 60), "Rain" (p. 63), "Sandpipers" (p. 66), "At Majority" (p. 73), "I'm Here" (p. 74), and "The Green Shepherd" (p. 82), copyright © 1956, The New Yorker Magazine, Inc. "Rain" (p. 63), copyright 1956 by Howard Moss, is reprinted from *A Swimmer in the Air* by Howard Moss with the permission of Charles Scribner's Sons; this poem first appeared in *The New Yorker*, "Letter to an Imaginary Brazil" (p. 64) is reprinted from *The Hudson Review*, Vol. IX, No. 3, Autumn 1956 (copyright 1956 by The Hudson Review, Inc.) and from *A Swimmer in the Air* by Howard Moss (© 1957 by Howard Moss) with the permission of Charles Scribner's Sons. "III. Mutterings Over the Crib of a Deaf Child" (p. 98) and "Lament for My Brother on a Hayrack" (p. 101) are reprinted with the permission of *The Sewanee Review*, and also appeared in *The Green Wall* by James Wright and are reprinted with the permission of the publishers, Yale University Press.

Stanford University Press, Stanford, California
London: Oxford University Press

Printed in the United States of America

Library of Congress Catalog Card Number: 49-49262

CONTENTS

POEMS NOT ENTERED IN CONTEST

POEMS ENTERED IN CONTEST

UNDERGRADUATE POETRY

Best Poems of 1956

THE SONG

So large a morning, so itself, to lean
Over so many and such little hills,
All at rest in roundness and rigs of green,
Can cope with this rebellious wing that wills
To better its obedient double quite
As daring in the lap of any lake,
The wind from which ascension puts to flight
Tribes of a beauty which no care can break.

Climbing to song it hopes to make amends
For whiteness drabbed, for glory said away,
And be immortal after but because
Light upon a valley where its love was
So lacks all picture of reproach it ends
Denying what it started up to say.

W. H. Auden

THE CHILD HERMES

A FIGURE IN A GARDEN FOUNTAIN

Child Hermes, clasp that tortoise on your shoulder,
The pattern of the Lyre,
Never to lose it, never to grow older
Or join the tuneless choir.

Still by your mountain cave the music lingers,
Where, as the neat-herds tell,
You found and tuned for all earth's after-singers
The first dark lyric shell.

Athene heard, Eros let fall his quiver,
Saw and remembered long
The grey eyes of the glorious wisdom-giver
Softening to hear your song.

So sweet the sound was that the listening Naiad
Hushed the still-rushing stream,
And in an open glade the Hamadryad
Stood in a spell-bound dream.

You lost that shell, and well you know the reason,
Look innocent as you may;
Sly rogue, I have watched you, in and out of season,
And seen the tricks you play.

You stole the sun-god's cattle, and Apollo
Flashed on you through the fern.
He bore your lyre to heights where none can follow,
And he will not return.

His was the blacker theft; he feigned to pardon,
And took the lyre for fee.
Only your silence in this moonlit garden
Pleads with Mnemosyne.

For here, at least, Mnemosyne draws near you
    With thoughts of that far Spring
When on the thyme-clad hills with none to hear you
    Your heart began to sing.

The nightingale remembers, and the roses
    Breathe out an air more sweet,
And in the dusk a water-lily closes
    White petals at your feet.

Lift up your leaden tortoise, hold it firmer
    Now in your leaden hand.
The gods who hear your own small fountain murmur
    Will smile, and understand.

Alfred Noyes

EPITHALAMION

Singing, today I married my white girl
beautiful in a barley field,
wise are her eyes so touch holy wood—
give my love to the loveless world
and all that is ours and gently good
to all the living but not the dead.

Now no more than vulnerable human
we, more than one, less than two,
are nearly ourselves in a barley field—
and only love is the rent that's due
though the bailiffs of time return anew
to all the living but not the dead.

Shipwrecked, the sun sinks down harbours
of a sky, unloads its liquid cargoes
of marigolds, and I and my white girl
lie still in the barley—who else wishes
to speak, what more can be said
by all the living against all the dead?

Come then all you wedding guests:
green ghost of trees, gold of barley,
you blackbird priests in the field,
you wind that shakes the pansy head
fluttering on a stalk like a butterfly;
come the living and come the dead.

Listen flowers, birds, winds, worlds,
tell all today that I married
more than a white girl in the barley—
for today I took to my human bed
flower and bird and wind and world
and all the living and all the dead.

DANNIE ABSE

BECAUSE I LIVE

Because I live—and you, not—
Waves that traveled the ocean of our years
On their long way to the edges of the world,
Shatter, broken, against that rock.

However much I had become
Terraced to vineyards and grown up to wheat,
A net of towns and roads across my heart—
I am compressed to one hard fact.

Stone does not stay bare stone for long:
The armored pine cone's seed discovers cracks,
Growth and forgetting generate new loam;
I meet an unexpected look or word
And all but break under orchard bloom.

EVELYN AMES

ON GETTING BACK TO AIRPLANE SPOTTING AFTER TEN YEARS: A SEQUENCE

I. THE HAWK

The brazen-footed hawk above the wood
Banks silently, and silently the sun
Tips beak and claw as with that creature's blood
Whose day was done before this day was done.

As he the ground, so we scan heaven for change,
Hawk's-eyed, yet groundlings chiefly—one with those
Who wait the stranger known as worse than strange:
A sudden air-born shadow dipping close
To merge impossible fantasy with fact,
To rend surprise in two and hold the prize
Before reaction can defeat the act
Or premonition show monition wise.

Here, bloodied only by sun, we stay
Awaiting that which does not come, but may.

II. CALLING IN

So the report runs, so the word is said
(The singing wire takes the short song best) :
"One plane, bimotor, low, heard overhead,
Out of the northeast, flying due southwest."
We do not say, "This is the kind of night
Wool makes a warmer blanket than the snow;
Three in the morning is no time to fight;
Suppose we call it quits, pack up, and go"—
Or, "Looking up, with hands bent round our eyes,
We could not see the monster for the sleet,
Though we have taught our ears to recognize
His gross, explosive, guttural, double beat."

We give direction, type, and height instead:
"One plane, bimotor, heard low overhead."

III. DOG WATCH

The transient dog who came to try our love,
Pre-empt our ancient armchair like a throne,
To curl his muddy curls beside our stove,
And lick our broken bread for lack of a bone,
Was one of those for whom the watch was kept.

What tramp, which brotherhood of monks
He represented where he laxly slept,
What savages, what children, or what drunks,
What tattered treasure in the terrible wind,
What snoring slumberer in another's bed,
What hapless innocent, what heedless hind,
We never asked him, and he never said.

Yet for his bootless joy, his fruitless right,
We stared the stronger through the transient night.

IV. TWO WORLDS

O life of silver in the lofty air,
Translucency of wings there, high, way high,
Deluge-descent of dronebeats falling where
We stand, way low, of earth, as they of sky:
We know their drift, though lacking downward look
On border sand beside the corduroy sea,
On wrinkled pasture ragged at the brook,
On movement merged to immobility.

Yet their monotonous eminence of place
Negates the lesser noise, the closer grain
Of what on earth we recognize as good.

We own the silence and enough of space
To seize, in trembling consciousness of gain,
The flight of deer within the flickering wood.

V. NIGHT WATCH: WINTER

Invisible above the frozen field,
Inaudible as ice in seams of stone,
In ruthless action inwardly revealed,
Once more the arrow wind barbs deep in bone.

The demon cold, dispassionately borne,
Accepts the tribute of our uttered breath
Vanishing fast above the ruined corn
Like a premonitory sight of death.

And down amongst the stubble, swept of snow,
The scattered vertebrae of animals lie,
Unwatching eyes, reproving from below
The warden stars in the perpetual sky,
Both powerless, being past power, to do what we
Conceive that task of vigilance to be.

VI. ALL'S WELL

Now ring the bell, call in the passing plane
Which carries home the signatures of peace.
Now close the door, domesticate again,
And revel in the softness of release.

Now scrape before your mirrors, build your roads,
And watch your children laughing in the sun,
Accept the here and now, follow your codes,
And do unto your neighbor what is done.

Yet know: beards grow, the jungle will encroach,
The unwatched child may stare beneath the wheel,
The near and dear recede, the far approach,
The neighbor-nation fabricate in steel.
Another hand may ring the watchman's bell,
An alien tongue proclaim that all is well.

CARLOS BAKER

SIR GAWAIN

Frost and new year pitched a white morning round him.
Swinging from the castle in a chime of sleet
His hooves pealed down the silver valley
Where girls with skirts in spate and foaming aprons
Fed geese into the wind, and waterfalls
Flounced down from pool to stone.

All that sharp year since his green enemy
Fastened on the fields and sucked them pale
His throat ached under the seasons like a vault,
The strong moth fidgeted in his eyelids. For a year
The wine ran through his cup like sand
And the boar's head mutilated his dreams.
His doom was each day's date, a bright
Malignant freckle on faint parchment.

And now he rode in the new year, where trees ran
With steady antlers beside the storm. The bridge
Lunged over the river into the green chapel.
But the ignis fatuus of a happy ending thawed
The icicle that kept his heart together,
The marrow of despair hissed out of his bones.
World and the winter cracked and free the grass
Jousted once more in the plains of the west country
As in the bright unravelling of spring
His banner bloomed again in Arthur's court.

PATRICIA BEER

GEMINI

They were both seed and stars, the twin gods.
Perched like gulls upon the mast of midnight
They kept their place above the listing earth
And led the Roman armies round the sky
And through the Forum in the days when names
Nested and sang in every monument.

In those days they were brightly dyed with time,
The gemini, like a leaf which is still green
Still crisp as an eyelash, though it fell
Dead in the blinking of a distant tree
A wind ago. They were both sap and ghost.

Even when they stiffened wholly into stars
The night still flowed under their golden ice
They left the Forum, but their broken names
Work roundly up through the soil in each dry season.

PATRICIA BEER

CATARACT

(I)

I walk to my Gethsemane with a heart
Shedding the name of light in syllables
Of faith. Forever is until the knife
Held by a gentle hand pierces the cloud,
Probes for the sun and writes with bloody words
The shape of hills, the faces of my friends,
The bright ramshackle pageantry of colour,
The pictures in the fire, the printed page.

Just for a little time and yet forever
Watch with me, Lord. There is a voice crying
That this would be a splendid time to die.
O God! forever is the dark minute
Forever is until the pyramids
Blow down and the dust settles on the sea.

(II)

When the bright bubble of a dancing dream
Quicksilvers through my bandaged head, the night
Is brighter than the day. But I must tread
A lonely path before I win my sleep.
My head stays on the pillow but I see
In my mind's eye, which does not play me tricks,
An altar-stone upon the mountain top
Solemn and silent as an empty Eden.

This is my pilgrimage. I place my pride
Upon the sacrificial stone. My eyes
Have coined the face of grief, they shape his name,
They still have tears, they know that in the dark
Direction of my prayer the light will break
Tomorrow or the next day or the next.

(III)

Say that my sight is blunted, that the world
Is dark for me, that there's no moon tonight.
Speak of eclipse and shadow, speak of dusk,
But if you love me do not say that word.
My mind is locked against the ultimate fear
That turning from a bleak dream I shall find
On lips not yet awake the unlovely black
Immeasurably unkind and lonely word.

From prayer to waking runs a stubborn dream.
There is a beach where it is always summer.
Sun shall not burn his head nor tide molest
The sea-child playing in the sand. The dawn
Dissolves my pain as I set out to find
That golden boy and bring him home again.

David Scott Blackhall

THE LAMENT OF ORPHEUS

Down to the kingdom of
The sudden gun, the thief, the grimy coin,
The gang, the shadowed interchange, the fist,
The rankness of the dark that took romance,
The unresponding death in which is found
The passion that is missing from the world.
There in the underworld that owns the dark,
In dirt I found the murdered strength they stole,
The intensity of lust that like a ghost
Takes on a murky shape to last a night,
The shamelessness that once was unashamed.
In that impersonality of night
I saw it but it would not come to life.
I said it would and told the darkness so,
But it cannot stand our ordinary air.
Is it that hearts, like scars, are red awhile
Only to turn white? The world and I
Knew this intensity but now no more
Because of what the night has done to it.
There in the night it lives on what is not.
There in the silence that is violence
It is buried by the bowels of the mind.
The strength of passion has gone underground
Where like the blackest secret it is kept.

EDGAR BOGARDUS

THE WALL OF ROME

Buses and motorcycles pour their noise
Through what was once great Hadrian Caesar's pride
And the reason that the wall retains its poise
In spite of all the city there outside
Is nothing more than history of course
Reminding her that once the umber homes
Beyond it would have been the first to fall
To those barbarians that plundered other Romes
Though now perhaps the most barbarian force
Is on the inside of the useless wall.

But why does she, a simple tourist here,
When she goes out beyond what kept Rome in,
Feel freedom suddenly as well as fear
At passing through it, why does she begin
To have the sense of plane trees and the smell
Of country bringing moods in which she yearns,
And why does passing through the wall provide
A comfort to her mind when she returns
Except that walls are walls with their own spell
And where they are do something for each side?

No modern city could, it seems, contain
Itself this way without the space to spread
Hurling out its anxiousness and pain
And is there something hidden in her head
To correspond to this great fragment where
A moment of her history occurs?
Whatever she might build would overflow
And yet she knows two portions are both hers,
A place of refuge and a place to dare,
And which the wall walls in she does not know.

That, perhaps, is why she likes the rules
And everything partaking of strict form,
Not that she thinks within such clumsy schools
To find a satisfaction in the norm

But that she, too, has her share of history,
The old triumphant moment when she hurled
Back every savage and invading urge,
And now she wants it as a place to see
And to be seen by others in the world,
A memory of strength through which to surge.

And should you find her proud and puritan
In what she may decide to do or say,
Is it merely to keep something in,
Trying in some old outdated way
To build around the mind a stone extent,
Or is it a part of that same broken wall,
A kind of token ring without much might,
Inside, not inaccessible at all,
But strong in spirit and magnificent,
Especially when it can catch the light?

EDGAR BOGARDUS

GREY OWL

When fireflies begin to wink
over the stubble near the wood,
ghost-of-the-air,
the grey owl, glides into dusk

Over the spruce, a drift of smoke,
over the juniper knoll,
whispering wings
making the sound of silk unfurling,
in the soft blur of starlight
a puff of feathers blown about.

Terrible fixed eyes,
talons sheathed in down,
refute this floating wraith.

Before the shapes of mist
show white beneath the moon,
the rabbit or the rat
will know the knives of fire,
the pothooks swinging out of space.

But now the muffled hunter
moves like smoke, like wind,
scarcely apprehended,
barely glimpsed and gone,
like a grey thought
fanning the margins of the mind.

JOSEPH PAYNE BRENNAN

FINAL STONE

No giant walks the final land,
no mountain towers, no wall;
no leviathan of sea and mind
withstands the brutal sifting of the tide,

What we live by in the end
is polished for the hand,
purified,
and small.

Final word and ultimate stone
lie on the sea's floor
with the grains of hills
and the shark's tooth
and the small ear-bones of whales.

JEAN BURDEN

AN INSCRIPTION FOR RICHARD EBERHART

I do not intend the people I know to believe me
outside themselves: belief is inside the self.
"It is the not-me in my friend delights me,"
Emerson wrote. It is my friend in me
that lets me see my friend. —These are convictions
one sleep this side of poetry. But in time,
with sleep dissolving from me like a mist
I find the shape of a scimitar still in my hand
and know what holy wars I would have gone to
in the right season. When I say to my friends:
"We *are* that invisible war," they smile
with a smile I know from myself. It is so we learn,
one from another, our difference is no war
but the delicate jointure of the parts of a skull.

But is the articulation of bones a meeting?
I have slept on ruined Rome and wakened green
with the squeal of birds and the power-hum of the bee
sealed in the air like amber. In the atrium,
a laborer was eating bread and cheese
in the noonday of his wine. I watched his ease.
It was longer than the ruin. "Bon apetito!"
I cried like God in the Sunday of my pleasure.
He raised his wine flask and called back, "*Salute!*"
Then did he turn to stone? Or the stones to him?—
Something stayed fixed in time out of that meeting:
a signal from my friend in me, a placement
of holy banquets in their atrium,
a vision of the bones that speak themselves.

JOHN CIARDI

FOR BERNARD DE VOTO

A thumb and a forefinger on the eyes
draws down the light: the fact that teaches all
shuts at the lid. That last hand, still in air,
not yet, nor ever, wholly returned from its gesture,
changes to a dead weight upon the heart.
Goodbye to seeing and goodbye from sight.

This was a man. This lump in the numb blank
of bedsheets, hours, losses. Like a tide
his warmth sinks from the mudedge of his blood.
His interrupted face above that tide
turns to a blue-veined marble one firm hour,
then shudders liquid to the end of time.

Wolves, eagles, fishes, angels—when they dared—
have died into that sea. Leviathans and cells
have burst from their stiff last across that mud.
So must a man be what the sea takes back.
But here, and for the man hour of a thought
it is an admiration stuns the sea.

What shall the sea in all its driven pumps
cast up from its pearl chambers in the sun
more than the man it takes? more than the run
of the infinite small waters of his brain
away from their stilled systems in the gulf?
To name a man is to give birth to nature.

Sea that drains all dregs, drains this. Goodbye.
This was a man, and I will swear his name
whole as I may from my own name and losses.
I knew no fault in his I could not love.
I find no death in us but justifies.
One deep is all, and its one shore—the man.

JOHN CIARDI

END OF THE ROAD

The color of October afternoon
Gave the light pause and lingered. Autumn sighed
A last and western breath. The sidelong moon
Dim in the aster sky seemed great with tide
Growing to spring in evening, and our ride
Across the river, climbing with the trees,
Had stroked to silence all but the brute stride
Of engine firing to its own decrees
Yet underfoot, locked in, and self-consumed like a
disease.

We had come through in stealth along a road
That weather wrinkled. Time had stood apart
To watch the trees take back what men had owed
And lapsed in death and debt. A land too hard,
Too grudging, broke them, ending with the heart.
And we went there, smooth on our springs and tires,
Past graveyards seeming laid there from the start
And holes of houses fallen, whose desires
Would darken had they stood, ringed with rugosa
briers.

And autumn paused where the road had met an end
In a house grown like a grave and standing still.
I killed the rage of engine with a hand
And we set foot on earth. Time had our will,
Autumn our heart. An air flowed down the hill
And loosened leaves that flittered in the light:
The house grew darker as the gathering chill
Whitened the moon and touched the pines with night,
Biding a time, a fall with all its winter weight.

We moved. The windows gathered in our shade
But gave back nothing. We were there alone
In an emptying air, called by a world inside,
Treading unbalanced on the threshold stone

And low behind us an impending moon
That spent its light upon each wasted pane:
The year, the day and light, all we might own
Of mortal seasons, failed in that dying lane,
And we turned back, our headlights sifting
    the night like rain.

Louis O. Coxe

ASCENDING PARALLELS

Now is the summer solstice when the ants
Must run the seasonal invasion
Of man's private patterns and precise
Arrangements.
From the closed and neuter darkness
Of obedience,
The antennae, lifted,
Accept the way of martyrdom
Down the unguarded crevices
To my spilled sweet, my inadvertent
Crumb.

And yet, to deal with them, I cannot stoop
To machinations of the poisoned honey. I
Am too aware
How wide the gate is I have left ajar
For commerce with my own necessities, so that
An easy camouflage could well insinuate
Within my avid citadel
A lethal nostrum.
I cannot crush beneath my feet
The animation of that striving dust,
Its mercy prayer
Unformed, its doom

Too far in its immensities
For apprehension.
Rather, I will skirt
That little business there across the room,
Thinking how a time may come
When thunderous steps will move (with care,
I hope)
Among the blind wheels of the galaxies,
And, also, spare.

GEMMA D'AURIA

STREET OF MASKS

Let slip the midnight mask and ask me in
for the cuffs of my world are frayed
and in this street fog-muffled shapes avert their faces
(tissue of ice on stone and echo of departing).

Let slip the mask for I need the fire of your eyes
and my breath will rosy the midnight cold of your hand
this street where we pass looms gaunt and a year is dying
(sleet on the lips and a lost bird's lost gray feather).

I will drop my mask when you ask me in
for under the eaves your room is chill
and I will not notice the smell of mould in the passage
(fear at the door and the hours like nooses hanging).

Here in the street where we pass and have passed
since time began, with our masks for armor
(ice on stone, sleet on lips and fear in the doorway)
let us slip our midnight masks and enter a morning.

ALAN DONOVAN

THE FORERUNNER

In the scorched places between Kedron and the
Dead Sea,
in the birdless land hummocked with pallid clay like
the heads of lepers,
satyrs blinked at him from orange rocks,
ghouls spat at him from the carcasses of camels
when that scarecrow man Jokhannon
wandered the gritty waste.

He too met the Tempter.
When he roamed pitted hillocks
seeking honey in the grey towers of the bees,
little imps—coneys with faces of pale girls—
lisped at his heels.
When he prayed voices assailed him, hissed from
the dust-whirls,
roared blasphemies from the corrugated mountains,
the bitter pink ravines
where the bad jinn have their spectral castles,
doors opened in the air, spinning vortices of negation.
Sometimes mirages promised palaces and lakes,
flimsy gardens falsifying sand,
sweet whisperers, sweet odours, rose and spice,
stole through his sleep,
and worst of all Hell's lures,
would often come tripping towards him, two by two,
twelve ingratiating devils
in the appearance of young men and old who cried,
"Hail, Master! Hail, Messiah!"

But powers of the air cannot prevail with one
who hears the horn of judgment in his secret ear,
who feels the feet of the expected One
walking along the jordans of his blood!

So John saw the appointed day rise over the
    horns of the mountains.
Light danced like angels along their crests
as the Forerunner went striding city-ward
    through the waste,
a dry wind shaped like a man, a walking voice,
a lion who cleared a pathway for the Lamb,
a thorn who knew he only foretold the Rose,
great cock of God who warned of the rising Sun
lest men should wither by its sudden fire
lest men should perish from the shock
    of unprecedented Love.

LEAH BODINE DRAKE

THE WEEDS AND THE WILDERNESS

O let them be left, wildness and wet,
Long live the weeds and the wilderness yet.
GERALD MANLEY HOPKINS, *Inversnaid*

After you pass Owl's Candle and Pickporridge the lane tilts
to Marry-in-the-Up, where a stone barn burrows
into the steep side of the Pickpack, lording the Waver valley.

Follow the cranky path and you come out upon Pickpack
Heath,
magenta with heather in flower, or coppered with bracken,
squatting like a gipsy in rainbow rags above the tidy hedges of
the vale.
Here the track walks by itself
between abrupt pools of ancient clay-pits, their cobalt water
cloddy with cloud-shadow,
and ends at Brock's Clump where the old barrow humps in the
ling
and five haggard pines, with their orange trunks rooted in
giants' bones,
knuckle together against the huffles of wind.
This is the high place, the house of hare and whimbrel.
No one comes or goes.
Only at dusk a fox will slip like a rusty ghost among the thistles
and broken stones
or a badger lumber to his sandy holt under a snarl of bramble.
From here you can overlook the brooky lands from Hern Plash
to Puddleswick
where the Waver loses itself in marshes, and the basket-
willows
drown their Ophelia-hair in little sly streams.
There the lanky heron feeds among the sedges and bayard moss
or flaps silently, like a thought through an unfretted mind,
over Rockinglass and its quaking sands to the hidden ponds of
Dragonsholm and Pendragon,
far as The Slake itself where the mud wears tidewater like a
skin.
This is the wet kingdom, the house of ooze and rush.

Heath and gorse, marsh and moss, the sandy, the sodden . . .
these are the uncouth places that planners of garden-cities do
not love.
They are not concerned with man and his notions.
They exist only for themselves and for that human few
who need the world's tart as well as honeysweet
and feel most at home in such unhomely wastes.
They will go some day, I suppose,
the heather uprooted, the badger killed with his kindle,
even the flats drained for corn and emptied of hern.

So let me hold in my mind a day when summer blurred to
autumn, when I walked
from Owl's Candle over the umber ling of the Pickpack to
Brocks' Clump
in a warm, gusty drizzle, with a sky of smoky pearl.
In wild air that smelled of wet pine and fern
I stood to my knees in burnt-gold brake that dripped with
pendles of rain,
and saw below me a swan rise from the wickers of Hern Plash
with a squeak and brattle of wings,
and fly over to Rockinglass through a sudden dazzle of sun.

LEAH BODINE DRAKE

A LETTER FOR ALLHALLOWS

I am still hurt, Plin,
by your desertion. Now and again,
between rains, or among
sagged syllables on a page,
I am stopped by your grinning, lantern-jawed,
monkey-eared, beautiful face.
And I am hurt
because you went to war
and died right in the middle of your letters,
and never said goodbye.
And then your father followed you,
at a respectful distance,
and the great house on the hill
went for a Trappist monkery.
I hope those monks
have veneration for the juniper
and the blackberries and the frog pond
and the dust of toy soldiers in the attic
where we warred long November afternoons;
above all, for the black road that,
if I listen on All Souls' Eve, will clatter
to the gait of you riding home from the white woods
on Diamond, your horse.
The glue is long since dry
they made of him. But we mark well
he was the last of the historic horses:
Revere rode him, and Sheridan,
and Sitting Bull.
I hope the monks treat you gently, shades
galloping alongside the empty meadows,
from Concord and Lexington,
the fords of the Shenandoah,
forks of the Little Bighorn.
Surely they would not be unmerciful
and frighten away with signs and bells and torches
so young an old soldier and his friend,
who, one way or another, were made ghosts
in all their country's wars.

PETER KANE DUFAULT

THRUSH SONG AT DAWN

Bird song is flute song and a glory
Of the morning when the sun unascending
Holds his other glory of mentality

And the dawn has not the mental mockery
But the birds from sweet subconscious wells
Pierce through all barriers to sense,

They send and giving sing divinity,
So sweetly charged with subterranean meaning
They are like angels in the morning

Come from ancient time, a fast enchantment,
To bless our mortal songless weakness
And trail a vocal glory all the day.

I would not be a bird, but I would hear
Deep in some lost purity, beneath the mind,
There in the sweet, dark coil of time,

As in a mother, the thrush as savior,
And a sovereign mediator; or any other
Lung-red singing: Richness propounds confusion,

That pleasure that will never cease to be
Where we are played upon without a fault
By magic tones we love but do not have to know.

RICHARD EBERHART

THE WINESHADE ESSENCE

In the arbor of my childhood,
green morning my roofage,
deep grapes like a midnight
sombered the leafage.

In the arbor where my childhood
afternooned and thirsted
for liquorlumpy fruitage
shadow-treated, dusk-frosted,

where clusterfall midnight
splashed the slatted arbor,
I ate gross purplings,
I drank vine-vapor.

In that arbor-calm childhood
I cut green capers
toward king-colored bunches,
to royal high purpose.

In a yard with an arbor,
those reap-ready seasons,
I sucked along of childhood
the wineshade essence.

Norma Farber

JESU, JOY OF MAN'S DESIRING

(CHORALE FROM CANTATA NO. 147, BY J. S. BACH, ARRANGED FOR PIANO BY MYRA HESS.)

Ivory in her black, and all intent
Upon the mirror of her instrument,
Doubling her beauty to the eye and ear,
My Muse arranged this in a distant year.

I thought my longing then could not abide
The discipline to place me at her side
Whose love and art were joined without defect,
Luxurious touch and sway of intellect.

Korê and lady, Myra, downward glancing
Over the hand that sings to the hand dancing,
Breathe and be present now the shades grow still.
Sweet air, be figured at your mistress' will.

As he of Brandenburg hummed in his heart,
The tenor and the alto, part by part,
Mounted in joy amid the tranquil choir
To dwell but tenderly on man's desire.

Softly that note fell, for the baby burning
Under the wintry sign of his sojourning,
The westward star, lay upon Eden's breast
Where husbandman and hunter seek to rest.

So voices woke from every falling voice,
Bidding the Gentile and the Jew rejoice,
With all that generations may conceive,
In Miriam, who is the grace of Eve.

Had she not borne the seed of the Lord God
To ripen in her splendid belly's pod?
And who but sages of the fragrant East
Dared his epiphany, adorned the feast?

And how but in the Cyprian's tongue went round
The tidings of great joy upon that ground
And peaceful glory promised in the air?
Holy became the rose our bodies bear.

So ran Kapellmeister's hymn unending,
So dreamed the maiden on his word attending,
So, as I cherished her in my degree,
The page of ancient music fell to me.

Now life has turned and all seems far and late,
I find this luminous, and meditate
To praise again, though East and West are wild,
The girl, the singing, and the Christmas child.

ROBERT FITZGERALD

INWARD MOMENT

By the tilt of your face, by the whimsical look and the frown,
By the growths that surround us, the willowy ones and the
oaken,
By the weight and awareness of words, be they breathed or
unspoken,
In the surge of the senses pursuing the ultimate noun:
From Marseilles to Calcutta to name your enchanted own town,
A man is a tenuous thing, a deliberate token—
By what welter of winds, by what beautiful bright and
unbroken
Skylight did matter take eyes and the elements drown
In this bloodheat, these skeletoned bones, this alert and intent
Surveying and moving across the elastic terrain?
By what will were these clusters of pulsating images lent,
With such inklings of love to provoke in the hub of the brain
An austere recognition and gladness of utter assent
That a man holds the ingathered world as his deeded domain?

GERHARD FRIEDRICH

VINCENT

First there was nothing but his own wrist
To rage at—that it could go on fumbling
What the eye's glare thrust at it:
Earth walking, or a bunch of fingers
Coarse as the food they preyed on
Yet in the raw lamplight hopelessly alive.

Then the thirst for colour:
For a blue so clear it would be not paint
But water any woman of Arles could rinse
Her clothes in; or the incessant search
For a yellow you could hammer like the slain tree
Of a drawbridge, of a bed, floor, chair.

And with that, the struggle to keep everything in place
At once: the fight to hold the chair at bay
While bed and floorboards reared at each other
In their agony, till, a truce signed,
They could league their forces to reject this copy
Of a lost chair from their completed world.

Perhaps it helped to have people there.
If the bigboned face of a woman in a café
Could be stilled, even for a moment, in the modelling
Of cheek, throat and shoulder, life
Could be contained at least, no longer spouting
Cypresses or whirling an intense sun.

But in the end fields that he had maddened with
    the fury
Of his eye broke loose. Wheat's brightness
Sang like a swarm of bees in his shorn ear;
Crows spawned in an ocean that had smeared
The sky out, and the contorted earth
Howled its triumph through the plowed furrows of
    his mind.

RONALD GASKELL

UNDER THE SILENCE

A white slant of silence shaped the walls
Grayed beyond gray, grain long gone unto harvest,
Milled on the strong, stone grind of the wind.
There was the doorstone, deep troughed with honing
Steps of men long since made spirit. I
Have met them there, men whose gait and gesture
Strain through my veins, whose easy cast of thought
Catches sometimes still on strayed twigs
Of my dreams. There I came across their tread
Men once of substance, spiritless, as ghosts.
They took my passage unresisting, not as spirits
Drawn from childhood, sticky and sweet
In candied memory, and from our meeting
Rose clear communion, springing out like water
Still boiling from the rock. A strange speech theirs,
Not reaching from the frozen caverns of the dead,
But hanging like blossom between us just
Under the silence. There was no chiding among us,
No rebuke or warning, only the feeble wonder
That one so enlightened should stand so in the dark.

Yet I smelt their reproach—around the barn
Leaning over the years with no fatness to spill
From its lofts, only a skin to shed in
Eavesdroppings on deaf ears—the reproach
Of Humility that gives everything
Because it has nothing to withhold
To Pride that withholds everything
Because it has nothing to give.
The reproach hung in the smell of dust
Moldering under the eaves. I did not look again
Inside the house at leprosy of plaster
Disfiguring the straight-ribbed walls, for fear
I should feel again the contagion of kindred blood.

ROBERT GIBBS

SPARROW IN THE HOUSE

Does the rain's wide curtain lift? Wind bangs the door
And the sparrow is suddenly in the room like an actor
Whose role is violence and pain.
At first his terror flies from wall to wall
Looping the wires of fear among the chairs and tables.

But the looking-glass flames as if with ice
Or lilies in the lamp's day-colored sun.
He sees the gardens flash beneath its snows,
He sees the glittering cliff gape open—
The mirror's pure cascade admit him.

Meeting reflection's deceit again and again,
His image beats at the brink of scattering noon;
The flight of its hanging gardens, terrace on terrace,
    cries:
Shall you not, like the water ouzel,
Fly home through the cataract?

The hollow landscape shines without tarnish of
    imprecision.
Ten feet inside, the perfect lilies float excusing
His need to be real again in a real element.
But the hard clear glass hurls him off.
Let him out who leaves me no feather but fear.

Rosamond Haas

MATRIX

The sun is dying like a martyr's torch,
And all the clouds go down like hooded monks.
The waters yield their estuarial flame;
The mother night that made us comes to calm
The gentle perturbation of those waters.

We feel a faint affinity for night
Because we know that's when we were conceived.
We feel a bond with egg and seed and pod,
With bud, cocoon and larva, root and spore,
Wherever life is waiting to begin.

A lost bird cries, importunate and wild:
A hurt song against the throat of night.
In thickets reedy insect urgencies
Still ply their little victory over death:
They will create their kind before they die.

No lost or homing bird has ever thought
Of night as something to be tortured by,
As we do, insular and full of quest,
Beneath a mindless audience of stars,
Or under winter's pauper auspices.

THOMAS L. HARRIS

"REMEMBER THEE? AY, THOU POOR GHOST"

". . . read me,
Do not let me die . . ."

Edna St. Vincent Millay,
THE POET AND HIS BOOK

Such service as the quick may do
For those who lie beneath the frost
I do, this autumn dusk, for one
Whom only in her song I knew,
But loved therefor, and more than most
Whom daily I may look upon.

Finger at page, I think of her
Who raged that man goes down to dust,
Who grudged the mongrel Death a bone,
Yet knew he crouched against her door
And fed him from her hand, at last,
At midnight, in the house alone.

Oh, if in truth you wake and weep
For what Death took into the grave,
Poor grieving ghost, be comforted—
How little Death can take, and keep,
He knows, while from this book is shed
The lovely light your candle gave.

SARA HENDERSON HAY

TO THE GREAT LOVER

O Love, support me over burning stones
And shield me from the stream where I would drink—
The throbbing stream of life, lest I should dip
One disobedient finger-tip and sink
Below the pinnacle of Your embrace.

O Love, my course is set above the stream;
My feet are on the rock; my eyes discern
The sun wherein I burn; I dare not dream
Of water smoothing down this granite face.

Each blinding day of light, each blinded night
Must be endured while I am Yours to die
To this weak body and its strong desire.
Earth-rooted like a tree, I sweep the sky
To wrench my roots from where their strength is set.

Yet still I hear the stream, the moving leaves,
And the primrose wind that breathes of pagan Spring
Till the primal satyr in my nature grieves
And listens to the song it dare not sing.

O Love, a little while and I will know
What country shines beyond my glimmering faith;
Though now there is so short a way to go,
I need Your strength to fill my lack of breath,
Your love for all the loves I must forego,
Your life to lift my soul beyond its death.

PHOEBE HESKETH

CARRY ME BACK

The big blue jean, the summer-bored boy next door,
Has been marching through Georgia all afternoon.
Tramp, tramp, tramp on the piano, his fists have trod
The vineyard where my grapes of wrath are stored.
He has brought Johnny marching home again, again,
And tented on the old camp ground tonight once more.
I am a captive audience, neighbor slave to noise.

One-fingered, he wanders way down the Swanee River,
Where his heart, like mine, that's where it's turning
Ever. He asks the key of F, C, or G to carry him back.
Carry me back to ole Virginny (now it's both hands)
Where the corn and taters grow, beyond this hot
Suburban house, family, no school, no job, no fun.
Back to what I used to banjo my way back to—
Andersonville, Gettysburg, the decks of the Monitor.
Gone are the days, but we hear the voices calling.

By way of Brady's camera, when I was this boy's age,
I wanted to creep near Lincoln and the chin beard,
Through my uncle's stereopticon, to Grant's staff tent,
And hear that posed group break it up and talk,
Lincoln to Brady, Grant to Lincoln, the wrinkled
generals,
Belted and bewhiskered, to one another and the dog.
I'd be there, in a forage cap, with a long bayonet
Fixed to my long rifle, and my own cartridge belt.
I'd stand guard, a sentry, overhearing history.
I wanted to get aboard that iron-turreted Monitor
Below decks—Brady never did—and into timbered
trenches,
Those snug play places in a home war that made sad
songs.
Old Black Joe. Old Abe Lincoln. Old Virginny.
Old camp ground. Old boy next door, and old me.

John Holmes

THE MUSIC OF SOCRATES

Moving uneasily in his chains
He listened to the silence of his thought
And to the wind that whispered through the night
Of the returning ship from Delos.
He closed his eyes, and darkness quickly grew
Within the hollow of his head. Then like a flower
There rose the golden shape of Apollo's lyre.
A hand began to play, not Apollo's hand
But the hand of Dionysus, and the strings
Were lines of glittering flame, and Wisdom sang
With joy like the bird of Zeus
Perched in the branches of an immortal tree.

When morning came
He was a shadow to his ecstasy.
He talked in sober tones, yet every word
Danced like the sun upon the tumbling waves
Of his music. Hearing his reason
Burst into beauty, as a Silenus figure
Reveals the image of the God within,
His friends were moved with pleasure and with
pain
At his approaching death. The music filled the
room
And young Apollodorus cried and laughed
By turn, until he heard the words of Socrates:
*Many are the thyrsus bearers, but the inspired
are few*
Who, purified, can end the bitter round
Of entrances to this shadow World.

But Crito, who had offered up a bribe
To allow his beloved master to escape
Knew it was all in vain. The ecstasy
Of rightness and of death lay on the man,
And all his violence would do no good.
For Crito could hear no music in the air.
Only the indignant crowing of a cock
That he would offer to Asclepius.

MICHAEL IVENS

FOR MY YOUNG BROTHER

I think, as autumn comes tawny out of the tiger hills
and the ditches are piled with a ruin of color,
how we live in a November world
and the sun swings low in our sky—
even we, whose years should spell spring
and whose country, so the books told us,
was a young giant stepping among new hills
on a road of his own free making.

The frost has a bitter taste;
smoke is no longer the rollicking smoke of bonfires;
the freezing ground has an iron clang;
and what shall I say to my young brother
who gallops beside me as boys do
but somehow has not quite the look of a boy?

I shall dare to say, you must expect a winter,
but we can make an end to winter
and all these snowmen with their more than broomstick
guns;
and the spring, if we make that too,
will be such a spring as boys have never known,
with the Andes, the Ganges and Greenland just next
door,
with all the wheels turning by summery hands,
and no more hunger, and no more fences.
The very frogs will add a new note to their chorus
under the nearer stars.

MIRIAM JANS

GIFT OF TONGUES

Imagine now the simple table laid,
The bottles full of wine, the loaves of bread,
And the one woman coming and twelve men
Not as to that last supper when great doubt
Was washed away and finally cast out:
Visions were past now and their lives began

Again, had to be lived in usual ways
In new simplicity with all the blaze
Of glory passed into a chafing dish.
Their lord had risen and they waited for
The promised word, the message to restore
Aspiring souls back to the naked flesh.

At first they talked of ordinary things,
Not the great days now gone but gatherings
Of men who sought an order to their lives.
Then suddenly their speech became confused,
They spoke of things they did not know, they
    praised
As a man praises his new-found beliefs.

Yet they grew strange to one another, stared
At faces unfamiliar now. The word
That each man found was made for him alone.
The broken bread lay by each plate uneaten,
The flasks of wine stood by untouched, forgotten.
The easy friendship of the meal was gone.

Each man rode on the skill of his own tongue
As children do who take a foreign song
And shape their lives within its rise and fall.
Each was enlarged by language and went out
To test his eloquence beyond, to shout
And make great silence subject to his call.

So each went on his way and spread his speech
And marvelled at the sound of words, the rich
Music that held the people. Yet there was
Such distance between words and what they spoke
About, the marvels would not stand but broke
Away. This language seemed no fitting place

To hold a glory known, for words stay still
While myths burst out of languages they fill.
'This is no way to share the peace we knew'
They said, 'We must find silence once again.
Only a faithful silence can contain
The mystery we watched.' They went back to

The place where all the leaping tongues had come
Where now was shadowed silence in the room.
The story that they preached was sheltered here,
Not in the echoes of their garrulous speech
But in the sudden moment held when each
Could not distinguish ecstasy from fear.

ELIZABETH JENNINGS

REPORT ON THE SITUATION

To woman, a man will speak a kind of a truth,
But never all that he knows; for there's that
Which denies the fullest sharing, completest trust.
It's partly the mother-shape; and part the fact

That this opposite creature of such unaccounted variety
May not be thoroughly known—in an inmost corner
May harbour the hidden wish, or express anxiety
In an entirely unsuspected area.

So that all matters of love must resolve in truce
While the parties parley and meet on a no-man's-land,
Feign ignorance that so much of push and thrust
Was planned to carry the enemy's death in hand.

Then, like two countries, they may lie down quiet,
At something called a Peace, with borders drawn
Separating, intact. Each dreams by night
Waking victorious with the salient dawn.

All they can know is what agreement means.
Speaking with words, there's yet another language
That hands express, that action will design
Showing how single is their mutual voyage.

LOUIS JOHNSON

CONSIDERATION OF THE GYRES

If Yeats was right, we've 45 years left
Before this worn-out, overworked machine
Grinds to a standstill and the dark recurs;
But can it be so simple, dear,—our deft
Hands lapsed because a sage has seen
Visions of wheels among his Autumn fires?

Doubting, we sit, and fathom out our hope,
Playing for time against what's cruel and real
Within the ringing of his mushroom words
That cloud tomorrow's sails, or foul the rope
On which we'd walk to succour. Better steel
Oneself for truth—accept—and move towards

That hidden, waiting, neolithic morning
That dawns upon the mouth of some new cave,
Where such as you—coarse-pelted in the cold,
Troubles no Abstract; cooks, observes the warning
Of storm in cloud, and thunder that will prove
God's voice is still as terrible as of old.

And such as I will crouch beside the fire
Sensing therein no more than what's to eat—
No vision of the towers that marked the past—
His only cycle, that unwound desire
They measure lengthwise with their bodies' heat
Blind to the powers, patterns that hold them fast.

And just as they—with all our culture's pride
Riding to error, undenied decay—
We grope towards each other, kiss, lie down
Baffled by what we dream or know—and hide
From fury in that living-warmth—and play
At being innocent with what tricks we own.

Louis Johnson

TO BE BLACK, TO BE LOST . . .

Ask night how it feels to be dark,
to be pitch, to be black, to be lost . . .
ask winter the feeling of cold,
the bitter edge of frost.

Ask day how it feels to be light
exposed so that all may see
through the sharp lens of the sun
the glare of intensity.

With fears that torture the dark
and days that are rimmed with pride,
ask me how it feels to be both
exposed and doubly denied.

HANNAH KAHN

WE GATHERED IN THE YARD

We gathered in the yard and watched;
The clouds came up behind the wood;
My father dared to hope for rain;
We children, near him, understood.

The corn reached up, the wind came down;
The moment neared, the weather cock
Swung nervously on its one leg,
The barnyard gate broke from its lock.

A hollow din of withered leaves
Moved in a wall of stinging air;
The promise came, the promise stood,
The promise passed and left us there:

The clouds fell rottenly apart;
The empty wind went down the sky;
And when the sun came burning through,
My father turned his back to cry.

REEVE SPENCER KELLEY

SISTER

When ugliness meant so little,
It was easy to love the grotesque toy pig,
Difficult even to imagine the rutted wart
On an old man's nose.
Nor was it a matter of concern
That sister, a tom boy, was disliked
By most and always suspect of childhood's crimes.

In the end, more often than not,
She treated you meanly, which was expected
And guarded against, or loved you as a doll.
And always she was older and different from you.

But what I mean to say
Is that, with all of her flaws,
She was never ugly in any way, and this
Was apparent in everything, her movements,
Smile, apparent behind tirade and insult,
Grave bravado and utter thoughtlessness.

And what I am about, now, is that she grew
To be a sad and beautiful woman,
Was tormented no more or less than many,
Considerate to no great degree,
But beautiful.
It is that she died so recently
That I speak.
She is gone,
And there seems nothing between me, now,
And the wart on my nose, the pig grunting
Slothfully in the muddy patches of the mind.

SYDNEY KESSLER

AN ARUNDEL TOMB

Side by side, their faces blurred,
The earl and countess lie in stone,
Their proper habits vaguely shown
As jointed armour, stiffened pleat,
And that faint hint of the absurd—
The little dogs under their feet.

Such plainness of the pre-baroque
Hardly involves the eye, until
It meets his left-hand gauntlet, still
Clasped empty in the other; and
One sees, with a sharp tender shock,
His hand withdrawn, holding her hand.

They would not think to lie so long.
Such faithfulness in effigy
Was just a detail friends would see:
A sculptor's sweet commissioned grace
Thrown off in helping to prolong
The Latin names around the base.

They would not guess how early in
Their supine stationary voyage
The air would change to soundless damage,
Turn the old tenantry away;
How soon succeeding eyes begin
To look, not read. Rigidly they

Persisted, linked, through lengths and breadths
Of time. Snow fell, undated. Light
Each summer thronged the glass. A bright
Litter of birdcalls strewed the same
Bone-riddled ground. And up the paths
The endless altered people came,

Washing at their identity.
Now, helpless in the hollow of
An unarmorial age, a trough
Of smoke in slow suspended skeins
Above their scrap of history,
Only their attitude remains.

Time has transfigured them into
Untruth. The stone fidelity
They hardly meant has come to be
Their final blazon, and to prove
Our almost-instinct almost true:
What will survive of us is love.

PHILIP LARKIN

THE WAY TO THE SEA

The young men leave the country for the town.
And in the oozing rain they walk the street
Feeling the stones resentful of their feet.
Like beaked giraffes the agile cranes look down,
Hover above the agitated docks,
Bend, lift and beckon through the busy air.
Beneath them on the uncompleted hulls
Workmen like seed are scattered everywhere,
Spray paint, fling rivets, call to the swinging crane,
Ignoring the distant ocean and the gulls.
Slowly the ships grow, in the endless rain.

Under the beeches as the leaves swing down
Onto the unmoved water, where they lie,
In the mauve air among the smooth-barked trees
Whose branches chase a pattern on the sky,
The watchhouse has outlived its families,
Stares with starred windows as the children climb
Unhindered now upon the obstinate gates
(They would not open if you tried) to mock
The seep and patience of the stream that waits
To act its stately and frustrated mime.
Weeds film the water in the stagnant lock.

The river rounds the lock and makes its way
Unhindered through the darkening fields. The light
Seeks its chased surface. If a dead leaf drops
It floats upon the mirrored sky in which
Beyond the hawthorn and the naked beech
The rocks returning mark the hastening day.
The brindled waters redden in the gleam
As the sun sinks behind the autumn copse
And round the darkness curves the fading stream.

The Lagan leaves the country for the town.
Its unambitious waters slide between
Grey buildings bulking on the urban scene.

A smoky drizzle makes the city smart,
Damps the drab swans, and fills the powdered air.
The river empties at the wharfs and quays,
And spreads around the oily dockyard where
Crowded with passengers for overseas
The finished ships disturb it, and depart.

L. D. LERNER

POEM FOR A GOODBYE

When you go through
My absence, which is all of you,
And clouds, or suns, no more can be my sky,
My one dissembling will be all—
The inclusive lie
Of being this voice, this look, these few feet tall.

The elements which
Make me from our encounter rich
Cannot be uncreated; there is no
Chaos whose informality
Can cancel so
The ritual of your presence, even gone away.

You, then, and I
Will masquerade a lie,
Diminishing ourselves to be what can
Seem one without the other, while
A greater man,

In hiding, lies behind this look, this smile.
It's he who will,
Across sad oceans, meet you still,
Startling your carelessness with that once was.
His voice from this past hour will speak,
Cancelling Time's laws;
And in the world's presence his hand will touch
your cheek.

Foreign can be
Only that sound to you and me.
There is no thought that in its dying goes
Through such a region we do not
In it compose
Each other's selves, each in the other's thought.

You leave behind
More than I was, and with a kind
Of sad prevarication take with you
More than I'll be till that day when
Nothing's to do
But say, "At last," and we are home again.

NORMAN MACCAIG

WESSEX GUIDEBOOK

Hayfoot; strawfoot; the illiterate seasons
Still clump their way through Somerset and Dorset
While George the Third still rides his horse of chalk
From Weymouth and the new salt water cure
Towards Windsor and incurable madness. Inland
The ghosts of monks have grown too fat to walk
Through bone-dry ruins plugged with fossil sea-shells.

Thou shalt! Thou shalt not! In the yellow abbey
Inscribed beneath the crossing the Ten Commandments
Are tinted red by Fifteenth Century fire;
On one round hill the yews still furnish bows
For Agincourt while, equally persistent,
Beneath another, in green-grassed repose,
Arthur still waits the call to rescue Britain.

Flake-tool; core-tool; in the small museum
Rare butterflies, green coins of Caracalla,
Keep easy company with the fading hand
Of one who chronicled a fading world;
Outside, the long roads, that the Roman ruler
Ruled himself out with, point across the land
To lasting barrows and long vanished barracks.

And thatchpoll numskull rows of limestone houses,
Dead from the navel down in plate glass windows,
Despise their homebrewed past, ignore the clock
On the village church in deference to Big Ben
Who booms round china dog and oaken settle
Announcing it is time and time again
To plough up tumuli, to damn the hindmost.

But hindmost, topmost, those illiterate seasons
Still smoke their pipes in swallow-hole and hide-out
As scornful of the tractor and the jet
As of the Roman road, or axe of flint,
Forgotten by the mass of human beings
Whom they, the seasons, need not even forget
Since, though they fostered man, they never loved him.

LOUIS MACNEICE

THE REST HOUSE

The thick night fell, the folding table unfolded,
The black men cooked a meal on the thatched verandah,
The hissing lamp had hypnotised the lizards
Who splayed their baby hands on the wired window
While crickets fiddled and sizzled to drown the river
Who, bowling his agelong bias out of Uganda,
Was curdling and burbling his nightlong way to the rapids
Tipsy with goggled hippo and drifting lilies.

And on the dark the voices of unknown children
So shrill they might be white, sifted and splintered
And shrivered away till, noisy lamps extinguished,
The bed beneath the ghostly netting beckoned
To chrysalid or sepulchral sleep. But such
Was now the river's dominance that he filtered
Through even the deepest sleep, weaving his journey
Out of too little history into too much.

Louis MacNeice

THE ICEBERG

It is not its air but our own awe
That freezes us. Hardest of all to believe
That so fearsome a destroyer can be
So dead, with those lights moving in it,
With the sea all around it so charged
With its influence. It seems that only now
We realize the depth of the waters, the
Abyss over which we float among such
Clouds. And still not understanding
The coldness of most elegance, even
With so vast and heartless a splendor
Before us, stare, caught in the magnetism
Of great silence, thinking: This is the terror
That cannot be charted, this is only
A little of it. And recall how many
Mariners, watching the sun set, have seen
These peaks on the horizon and made sail
Through the darkness for islands that no map
Had promised, floating blessed in
The west. These must dissolve
Before they can again grow apple trees.

W. S. Merwin

CLOWN GETS GLAMOUR

Nights he swept the stars' great studio,
Climbed with his bucket through the tropic sky:
Lifting a ghost-sheet, half-suspicious, slow,
Stared in a camera's dark unanswering eye.

Would the world love and magnify his faults,
In the ground glass would he seem smooth, unbend,
And having turned successful somersaults
Walk out of the telescope at the other end?

Half taken with that image of himself
He moved around it, doing work once more,
Then raptly leaned across a velvet shelf
To scrounge a spare world unaccounted for.

Powdering in a glass they used to seek
The make-up of a star, he blinked to feel,
Sharp as the sneeze approaching, the unique
Incorrigible thrill of being real.

JOHN MILES

GENIUS LOCI

For a long while we did not know his name.
He was the boy we saw one afternoon
Hanging around the wharf when you and I
Went down to watch the Boston boat come in.
He stood in front of us, as grave and thin
As a child in a bad dream; but then as soon
As the old steamer whistled, he was gone.

Another time you saw him on the road,
Watching, you thought, the tracings in the air
Of a hawk's hover, beautiful and wide.
You saw him once astride somebody's wall,
With berries in his hand; and all one fall
He made the neighbor's field a passage where
The pheasants, flushed from hiding, filled the light.

I saw him once or twice, too, later on,
Surprised still by a loneliness as odd
And headstrong as our own. But when we learned
A little more about the place, you knew
And recognized him first by looking through
His strangeness to his eyes. He was the god
We call familiar now, and by his name.

SAMUEL FRENCH MORSE

RAIN

Dear, on a day of dumb rain,
When cats sleep and trees grow,
And, outside the windowpane,
Imaginary fish flow,
We, as lovers, lace our arms
Securely round each other's back,
Hoping to stave off lightning's harm,
To counter thunder's crack.

Then pleasure is as easy as
The body's closeness, and the mind's;
There is a kind of love that has
Them separate, but body finds
Body too tasteless without thought,
And lovers feel, when face to face,
That mere intellect falls short,
Short of an embrace.

Dwindling, the slim rain makes us seem
As green as any world that grows;
Intransitive in sleep, we dream
Ourselves curled tightly as the rose,
Whose bud we cannot praise too much:
This is the start of every song
That no philosophy can touch—
And only the dead are wrong.

Howard Moss

LETTER TO AN IMAGINARY BRAZIL

FOR ELIZABETH BISHOP

The pink tongues of certain flowers having
Only colloquial names (they are
So tough they might be used for scouring)
Stick out suggestively among green pods,
And the green's tough, too, though it surprises
The fingernail that frees its milk from fiber,
Running a white thread down the hand. One plant's
No menace, but from the plane, one sees
A writhing settlement that hides its danger,
Where snake and puma wrestle on a floor
Of sliding vegetation, and the macaw
May tear a scale off as loud and brilliant
As any virtuoso bending over keys
Of black and white—those colors missing here,
Where all is earth-green, earth-red, earth-brown,
And a sulphurous yellow takes the breath
Away from the breather, Elizabeth.

The waterfall, cruel as a kind of love,
Which, because it moves, is forced to cut
Some life away, is still a version of
The pastoral by being beautiful:
A dynamo that distance turns to song.
The mountain, too, has its deception—
Imagined stillness, though explorers lie,
Ironed out among its dark crevasses,
Where nature tries to wrest its forms from darkness:
Twisting, thickening spines and circles
Frightening the mind with a naturalism
That cannot weigh the difference between
A feather and a leaf. To fall asleep at night,
One thinks of nature as a human being:
The mountain a patriarch bending over life,
The waterfall a girl, stranded in a myth,
Whose tears have cut through rock, Elizabeth.

Though what is still may move, and come to grief,
Though what is moving stop, no longer safe,
I see you in your house upon a mountainside,
Lighting the lamps. When you look outside,
There is the room hung up between the mountains,
Reflected on the other side of glass,
And, swinging in that double cage of light,
The mind flies out to objects of its love
And finds impenetrable forms and shapes
That you can formulate when you pin down
Each butterfly of thought upon your board.
You'll see, as fine as fern, a single tree,
Which, sprouting all its foliage at once,
Will seem to move beneath a microscope
Until each cell is separate to the eye,
Thin-scaled as life upon the width of death,
Who cannot read your poems, Elizabeth.

HOWARD MOSS

SANDPIPERS

In the small territory and time
Between one wave and the next, they run
Down the beach and back, eating things
Which seem, conveniently for them,
To surface only when the sand gets wet.
Small, dapper birds, they make me think
Of commuters seen, say, in an early movie,
Where the rough screen wavers, where the light
Jerks and seems to rain; of clockwork dolls
Set going on the sidewalk, drawing a crowd
Beside the newsstand at five o'clock, their legs
Black toothpicks, their heads nodding at nothing.
But this comedy is based upon exact
Perceptions, and delicately balanced
Between starvation and the sea—
Though sometimes I have seen one slip and fall
From either the undertow or greed
And have to get up in the wave's open mouth,
Still eating. I have never seen
One caught; if necessary, he spreads his wings,
With the white stripe, and flutters rather than flies
Out to begin eating again at once.
Now they are over every outer beach,
Procrastinating steadily southward
In endlessly local comings and goings.

Whenever a flock of them takes flight
And flies with the beautiful unison
Of banners in the wind, they are
No longer funny. It is their courage,
Meaningless as the word is when compared
With their thoughtless precisions, that strikes
Me when I watch them hidden and revealed
Between two waves, lost in the sea's
Lost color as they distance me—flying
From winter already, while I
Am in August. When suddenly they turn
In unison, all their bellies shining
Like mirrors white with flashing signals
I cannot read, I wish them well.

HOWARD NEMEROV

THE ZOO

The elephant never forgets.
Africa sailed away
The forests burned
And all the streams went dry.
But as his great bulk turns
Within his tiny eye,
As if those wrinkles smiled,
The lowing song is heard.

The polar bear never forgets.
The arctic thawed apart
The water warmed
And all the cold fish died.
But as he roars alarm
And turns within his cage
His huge paws form
Their great applauding heart.

Even the turtle dove
Whose sky has lost its air
Does not forget
And from his wire bar,
Perched for that old wit
Of green and sun, stares out
On flying doves, and yet
Sings yet again of love.

ANTHONY OSTROFF

EARLY DUTCH

Manahatta . . .
A lovely name, he thought, and a lovely island,
lemon-lime in the filament of spring.
Only an arc of birdsong on the stillness
and curve of wing.

Clucking among the stones, a brook, translucent
through leaves like moons, through fluttering scarves
of trout.
Beyond the dogwood's crucifix, a rabbit
skittering in and out.

Manahatta . . .
A velvet word, he thought, and a velvet island,
like yielding moss, like lace on a fluted beach . .
A singing word in the mouth of a salty river
far from an old world's reach.

Here I would live forever, said Van Twiller.
Time does not move here, only the sun and sky.
Here I will drift through time like a lazy swimmer
and cities may pass me by.

JENNIE M. PALEN

GAME OF STATUES

In some far country where they must speak French,
The slow rivers forever shove
Carrying, reversed in blue, debris of birds
Bound outward, like travelers out of love.

Over pale drinks, the roses of the sun fall out.
In white or vivid black, gossip is kept
As that old bell in that old tower
Keeps the hour for an annunciation.

Hand held, hand extended
Never was intended to reveal
What, at a station or a quay,
The lover seems already not to feel.

We keep the hour,
Hand touching hand in tentative embrace,
Mock the bewitchment of the evening,
And wonder if this could be the place.

While careful of the hunter and the plain,
Tigers ripple slowly through the rain
Terrible to transients south of Spain.

Hand held, hand extended
Cannot be depended on to part.
As, by a bus stop or a tree,
The lover says with silence, "Stay with me!"

Talk to me now like Karen late one night,
Chewing her jewels and laughing at the silence:
"I cannot wait. I cannot hesitate.
"This time I'm certain there is no mistake."

Absent from love,
We flicker out and die.

The bell performs.

Caught between death and death,
We do not move.
Hand holding hand or reaching into shadow,
We fade with the light.

While on the dusky lawn
From the indifferent flowers,
A swift deer, cast into iron,
Leaps forever into troubled darkness.

RALPH POMEROY

MRS. B

I know—who does not?—Mrs. B,
Flushed from the ritual cup of tea.
The cigarette, the symptoms, and the chat,
The black serge skirt and nodding hat—
By these all ladies know
The gallant, tempest-battered crow,
This talkative, good-natured ghoul.

To every Mrs. A her Mrs. B
All ladies cool, all ladies fresh and cool
Hear her disreputable story
Of thieving tradesmen, sick relations,
Of suicide by gas, and operations.
She is their grim *memento mori.*

Under the shadow of her trailing skirt
Life's diurnal grease and dirt
Skulk about the kitchen floor.
Every Saturday at nine
She makes, on Dr. Death's front door,
The brass plate and the huge brass knocker shine.
All ladies cool, all ladies cool and mortal—
God keep them far from that conclusive portal.

James Reeves

THE FLAMING CAROUSEL

Round flies the flaming carousel
To rock and shock the screaming park,
The dizzy watchers one and all.
Who would not ride if it they could—
Those vaulting legs, that dancing wood—
Who would stand by in the dark?

There rides Fred and there Marie—
Close to the varnished necks they cling.
Their hair streams out (but where is she?)
Their faces blaze (and who is he?)
No one has caught the golden ring,
And still around those riders fling.

The music creaks, the flames die down:
Our voices rise above the sound.
Our eyes are spinning in a swirl
And cannot fix on boy or girl.
The flaming carousel slows down
And the charred children all step down.

Adrienne Cecile Rich

AT MAJORITY

When you are old and beautiful,
And things most difficult are done,
There will be few who can recall
Your face as it is ravaged now
By youth and its oppressive choice.

Your look will hold their wondering looks,
Grave as Cordelia's at the last,
Neither with rancor at the past
Nor to upbraid the coming time,
For you will be at peace with time.

But now, a daily warfare takes
Its toll of tenderness in you,
And you must live like captains who
Wait out the hour before the charge—
Fearful, and yet impatient too.

Yet someday this will have an end,
All choices made or choice resigned,
And in your face the literal eye
Trace little of your history,
Nor ever piece the tale entire

Of villages that had to burn
And playthings of the will destroyed
Before you could be safe from time
And gather to your brow and air
The stillness of antiquity.

ADRIENNE CECILE RICH

I'M HERE

(OLD LADY ON THE WAY TO SLEEP)

I

Is it enough?—
The sun loosening the frost on December windows,
The glitter of wet in the first of morning,
The sound of voices, young voices, mixed with sleigh bells,
Coming across snow in early evening?

Outside, the same sparrows bicker in the eaves.
I'm tired of tiny noises:
The April cheeping, the vireo's insistence.
The prattle of the young no longer pleases.
Behind the child's archness
Lurks the bad animal.

How needles and corners perplex me!
Dare I shrink to a hag,
The worst surprise a corner could have,
A witch who sleeps with her horse?
Some fates are worse.

II

I was queen of the vale—
For a short while,
Living all my heart's summer alone,
Ward of my spirit,
Running through high grasses,
My thighs brushing against flower crowns;
Leaning, out of all breath,
Bracing my back against a sapling,
Making it quiver with my body;
At the stream's edge, trailing a vague finger;
Flesh-awkward, half alive,
Fearful of high places, in love with horses;
In love with stuffs, silks,
Rubbing my nose in the wool of blankets;

Bemused; pleased to be;
Mindful of cries:
The meaningful whisper,
The wren, the catbird.

So much of adolescence is an ill-defined dying,
An intolerable waiting,
A longing for another place and time,
Another condition.

I stayed, a willow to the wind.
The bats twittered at noon.
The swallows flew in and out of the smokeless chimneys.
I sang to the edges of flame,
My skin whiter in the soft weather,
My voice softer.

III

I remember walking down a path,
Down wooden steps toward a weedy garden,
And my dress caught on a rose briar.
When I bent to untangle myself,
The scent of the half-opened buds came up over me.
I thought I was going to smother.

In the slow coming out of sleep,
On the sill of the eyes something flutters,
A thing we feel at evening, and by doors,
Or when we stand at the edge of a thicket,
And the ground chill comes closer to us,
From under the dry leaves,
A beachy wetness.

The body, delighting in thresholds,
Rocks in and out of itself.
A bird, small as a leaf,
Sings in the first
Sunlight.

And the time I was so sick—
The whole place shook whenever I got a chill—
I closed my eyes and saw small figures dancing,
A congress of tree shrews and rats
Romping around a fire,
Jumping up and down on their hind feet,
Their forepaws joined together like hands;
They seemed very happy.

In my grandmother's inner eye,
So she told me when I was little,
A bird always kept singing.
She was a serious woman.

IV

My geranium is dying, for all I can do,
Still leaning toward the last place the sun was.
I've tried I don't know how many times to replant it.
But these roses: I can wear them by looking away.
The eyes rejoice in the act of seeing, and the fresh afterimage,
Without staring like a lout or a moping adolescent,
Without commotion.

Look at the far trees at the end of the garden.
The flat branch of that hemlock holds the last of the sun,
Rocking it, like a sun-struck pond,
In a light wind.

I prefer the still joy:
The wasp drinking at the edge of my cup;
A snake lifting its head;
A snail's music.

V

What's weather to me? Even carp die in this river.
I need a pond with small eels. And a windy orchard.
I'm no midge of that and this. The dirt glitters like salt.

Birds are around. I've all the singing I would.
I'm not far from a stream.
It's not my first dying.
I can hold this valley,
Loose in my lap.
In my arms.

If the wind means me,
I'm here!
Here.

THEODORE ROETHKE

TWO CHILDREN

In that cold mountain climate after the swim
We climbed to the shed roof for our shivering.
To be a little closer to the sun, to steam
A little in his goodness, chattering
In our cold clinging suits and shrunken skin.

To be fanned out and dried in proper proof
Of his benevolence we climbed up close
Like morning glories to the lichened roof.

O what a shrine to bless our little veins
Like vines, our puckered skin and skinny flesh,
Our laid-out bones that stretched up splintery wood
To be a part of concentrated good

The shiver of wind, the cloud and shine, the drip
Of our long hair, and our cold patterns laid
On shingly slope strengthened the shape of God.

DOROTHY ROBERTS

AFTER FOUR YEARS

How to lay down her death,
Bring her back living
Into the open heart, the over-grieving,
Bury once and for all the starving breath
And lay down her death?

Not on love's breast
Lay down this heavy prize
And close at last the open, the gray eyes
Of her who in my woe can find no rest—
Not on love's breast.

And not in solitude
Lay the long burden down,
For she is there awake when I'm alone,
Who cannot sleep yet sorely, sorely would—
Oh, not in solitude!

Now everywhere I'm blind;
On the far journeys
Toward the magical old trees and cities
It's the same rooted sorrow that I find,
And everywhere I'm blind.

Is there a human prayer
That might unknot prolonged
Unnatural grief, grief that has surely wronged
Her very radiant presence in the air,
Is there a human prayer?

It is poor love, I know,
Mother and marvelous friend,
Over that final poverty to bend
And not remember all the rich life too:
It is poor love, I know.

"Rich love, come in,
Come home, my treasure.
All that you were and that no word can measure
Melt itself through me like a healing balm,
Rich love, come home."

And here lay down at last
Her long hard death,
And let her be in joy, be ash, not breath,
And let her gently go into the past,
Dear world, to rest at last.

MAY SARTON

AMERICA

The barns like scarlet lungs are breathing in
Pneumonia. The North wind smells of iron.
It's winter on the farm. The Hupmobile
That broke its back is dying at the fence.
At night in a thin house they watch TV
While moonlight falls in silence, drop by drop.

The country that Columbus thought he found
Is called America. It looks unreal,
Unreal in winter and unreal in summer.
When movies spread their giants on the air
The boys drive to the next town, drunk on nothing.
Youth has the secret. Only death looks real.

They never die. They go down with their hobbies
Into the basement, and are seen no more.
Enough, when something breaks, that widows mourn
"He would have fixed it. He knew what to do."
And life is always borrowing and lending
Like a good neighbor. How can they refuse?

LOUIS SIMPSON

THE GREEN SHEPHERD

Here sit a shepherd and a shepherdess,
He playing on his melancholy flute;
The sea wind ruffles up her simple dress
And shows the delicacy of her foot.

And there you see Constantinople's wall
With arrows and Greek fire, molten lead;
Down from a turret seven virgins fall,
Hands folded, each one praying on her head.

The shepherd yawns and puts his flute away.
It's time, she murmurs, we were going back.
He offers certain reasons she should stay . . .
But neither sees the dragon on their track.

A dragon like a car in a garage
Is in the wood, his long tail sticking out.
Here rides St. George, swinging his sword and targe,
And sticks the grinning dragon in the snout.

Puffing a smoke ring, like the cigarette
Over Times Square, Sir Dragon snorts his last.
St. George takes off his armor in a sweat.
The Middle Ages have been safely passed.

What is the sail that crosses the still bay,
Unnoticed by the shepherds? It could be
A caravel that's sailing to Cathay,
Westward from Palos on the unknown sea.

But the green shepherd travels in her eye
And whispers nothings in his lady's ear,
And sings a little song, that roses die,
Carpe diem, which she seems pleased to hear.

The vessel they ignored still sails away
So bravely on the water, Westward Ho!
And murdering, in a religious way,
Brings Cortez to the Gulf of Mexico.

Now Portugal is fading, and the state
Of Castile rising purple on Peru;
Now England, now America grows great—
With which these lovers have nothing to do.

What do they care if time, uncompassed, drift
To China, and the crew is a baboon?
But let him whisper always, and her lift
The oceans in her eyelids to the moon.

The dragon rises crackling in the air,
And who is god but Dagon? Wings careen,
Rejoicing, on the Russian hemisphere.
Meanwhile, the shepherd dotes upon her skin.

Old Aristotle, having seen this pass,
From where he studied in the giant's cave,
Went in and shut his book and locked the brass
And lay down with a shudder in his grave.

The groaning pole had gone more than a mile;
These shepherds did not feel it where they loved,
For time was sympathetic all the while
And on the magic mountain nothing moved.

Louis Simpson

FALSE SUMMER LEANS

False summer leans across the dwindling veins:
the crags are wild with flowers and dear indeed
the sails, green-leaved, that dizzy the blue waves:
and pleasant that boat's engine gravely humming
like Sunday pots on boil. The winter's pains
hang out like ragged washing, whitely streaming.

These are fine mornings when the boats at anchor
ride freshly painted on the winking waves
and sea-gulls, yellow-beaked, sidle down piers.
The herring surge into the clean Atlantic
and those who come with flowers to growing graves
are caught like bees within them, lost to tears.

Such music stirs within the naked rocks,
such waves remember where the dear heads range
studying water in a purer tide
that aging mouths gulp up the air like hawks:
for now indeed Time is no longer strange
but walks beside us calmly, groom and bride.

And this is much that, from the dizzied cliffs
descending late, we reach the level land
where growth as free as this can take our place.
This is a season we have never planned
but meets us gravely, face to equal face,
content to die nor seek to understand.

IAIN CRICHTON SMITH

CATHAY

The voyagers, who festered, made of it
rational end, season's surfeit past age
belled irritant from wharves on Tiber down
barrack- or brothel-talk, cabinet whispers,
an unelected muttering walking by waters.
There—centuries mounting fragments to belief—
it lay an inch further than probing fingers
on cobwebbed maps. All addings of one to one
made signally more than two. In deed, unlimited;
some vast, immutable, canvassed fragment.
Unbelief, like a guilty fascination, hampered
by sea the natural progress of their drift.
Fast deserts out of Aleppo, Pamir snow,
grassed Tartary lay between desire and real
(if the word is real) presence, perfected Cathay.
Falling alkaline down their throats enchafed
a year and a day of bitter swallowing pulled
mad in immensity at their world's far end.

Tremendously sane, their fictions grew.
Immutable, as desire or disease,
it hungered and hid in alien consciousness,
prospering out from its prohibitions
until resumed into a natural history,
probed, fingered, and exploited. Deliberate
mystery dies hard. *Is it true what they say,
soldier, about their women—you know?* You
have always known. Before recovery, unfounded
truth blew rashly through *their* seasons.
Discovered, indeed, how like unlikeness has to be,
and Cathay a liberating image, intricate
as a nest of ivory boxes, likeness multiplied.

KENDRICK SMITHYMAN

ON A PHOTOGRAPH OF A FRIEND, PETER WATSON (obiit 1956)

(DRAFT OF THE OPENING LINES OF A LONG POEM)

Dear scattered flesh, there was a moment
—This witnesses—when real light fell
Onto your features. They were. They sent
The image mirrors took for you along
Light-paths leading through an instrument.

In its black box, that snatched your opposite,
The sharp lens set you standing on your head.
A sensitivized surface remained white
Where no white reached it, from your eye sockets.
Dark it held your brow, touched by most light.

There in the camera's miniscule locked room
Your million-measured form changed into ghost
Negative in a microcosmic tomb.
Left-handed, soot-faced, values were reversed—
Blackness gleaming in a whited gloom.

Reverse of that reverse, this photograph
Through printed chiaroscura, looks up with
Your questioning ironic sad half-laugh.
Your gaze diagonal under grave lids,
Mouth still mocking—"This is all you have."

Yes. This is all we have. Yet like a beam
Patterning outspread leaves upon a wall
This harks back to the shoot from which it came.
You who are scattered now, were integral.
Proved, you once shining, and once whole and warm.

A galaxy of cells composed a system
Where one stood, in his kingly tower of bones,
His heart at his left hand: surrounding him,
The cycle of his tides of blood revolved.
Nerves, like antennae, pressed against a rim.

He moved, had density, occupied space.
Raised but his hand, and through the universe
Changed its relations there with every place.
Before his step, skies opened like a door.
Sleep took the seal of his intaglio face.

All this was you. And yet when you were there
I looked as with this camera's eye, you were
Print on my mind, as much as now you are,
Image reversed upon the retina,
Swivelled back by the brain, like the print here.

Shadows, I see, are all we've ever known.
Cabined in craniums our minds read upon
The instruments of senses objects shown,
Things turned to thoughts, that being thought are gone,
Across a screen where the brain waits alone.

All are hung round with gulfs and distances.
Loving, and being loved, is not to know
Each what the other's sole existence is,
The instant that has passed makes up for Now.
We are but present in our absences. . . .

STEPHEN SPENDER

A MEMORIAL, ENGRAVED IN WRITING . . .

A man's last journey should be like an afternoon's
Walk, an easy stroll towards rest, hands thrust
In pockets, a dog to heel, and the sun setting,
Something of himself about it. So William Morris
Went to his sleep, all he loved close around him,
Borne on the galleon-waggon, scarlet and blue,
Sailing under the full-fledged yellow elms,
And over the cottage gardens Michaelmas daisies,
Amethyst, rose-quartz, in their crystalline forms
Lying like seams of jewels, sparkling and shining
In loose stars uncovered to the rain.
As if splattered by a gigantic quill
Rooks blotted the sky, large jet bugles of birds.
Children leaned on gates whose lichen burned
In livid green and lambent amber, like toads.
And women, white aprons taut over rose or blue
Starched skirts, stood with summer at their back,
And the dark scrawl of winter written in a dark
Bare branch, and leaves that skittered like mice
    on the ground.
So, proudly, the yeoman and the craftsman
Travelled home with the creak of leather, the level
Hoof-fall, the beat of hobnails on a country road
For his last music, as apt for him as the thin
Cry of seabirds, the white, invisible flame
Hissing upwards to the sun as Shelley lay
The young, lost hero on his archaic pyre,
With the sea purring appeased, and the small waves
He loved leaping like kittens with sheathed claws.

MARGARET STANLEY-WRENCH

ALL SOULS' NIGHT

All Souls' night is a sad night.
Firelight, water and candlelight.
A bowl of water and walnut shells.
The shells are the boats of the dead. The souls
Of the dead are the candles burning.

In each shell a candle, the shells turning
This way and that in the draught, while the flame
In each burns silently down to the rim.

All Souls' night is a sad night.
Children's faces by firelight.
The quick and the dead, and the quick have lit
Candles in memory of the dead
And sail them in a bowl, a bowl of water.
And not in remembrance only.
For this night, this one night,
By firelight, water and candlelight,
They half believe that the dead return,
This one night as the candles burn,
And their half belief fills the room
Till the air breathes, till the dead come
To suffer again that passage of water,
The yearning moment of departure.
And of those that watch at least one
Is nearer to them than to the room
Of things and living. Hands reach to hold,
Hands draw her, her soul goes, cold
But befriended, out on to the water.
There's her metropolis. There streets are
Again places to walk in and those
Who walk beside her are those she knows.
The streets are lit there, lights burn
Comfortable at every turn—
She does not see the pavements lap
Black and silent under each step—
She would go now. I know she'd go.

I cannot hold her though I know
All of her mind. The lights draw her
And the soft undertow of water
And most the friendliness of the dead,
The being known and countenanced.

All Souls' night. We are all here.
Children's faces round the fire.
The beginning of the journey and the end.

We burn candles to defend
Our bit of time, but also to remember
That there is no defence. November
Comes. Stars faint now, air quite still.
Coming and going of souls. The defenceless will.

CAROL STEWART

"On All Souls' Night one scoops out walnut shells for the children, fixes tiny candles in them and floats them in the dark in a bowl of water.

WHEN WISHES WERE FISHES

Beyond your knees at Sailor's Glass
Boiled the kelp-smelling sea,
There the wind galloped in the tough grass
At the edge of the world, and our Sunday wish
At the edge of the world and free,
Was to bottle a dredged up jelly-fish.

Seaweed and dead fish and shells were lure
In the grave of the sandy bowl,
The glistening arms of swimmers struck
Sparks from the suncharged air, and a whole
Orphanage came down on the sand in a truck,
And old ladies were there for the cure.

All that clapping and smacking of gulls,
And that slapping of tide on rock,
Our senses twanged on the sea's gut string,
And the mother's cries, and the animals
That barked and charged, and the young ladies in a flock
Who ran the soprano scale and jumped the waves in a ring.

RUTH STONE

POEM

Your breath was shed
Invisible to make
About the soiled undead
Night for my sake,

A raining trail
Intangible to them
With biter's tooth and tail
And cobweb drum,

A dark as deep
My love as a round wave
To hide the wolves of sleep
And mask the grave.

DYLAN THOMAS

THE GALLOWAY SHORE

Sand white as frost: the moon stayed hard and high.
Far off, the lights around the Irish coast
Leapt up like salmon. A metallic sea
Chinked on the rocks. Within a shadow cast
By broken cliffs, a place of slippery stones,
I faced the speaking lights, small human signs
Of barren rocks and granite patiences.
Among the sounds of night a slithering wind,
Darkness of dark, in fitful cadences
Phrased the fresh world. There is no older sound.

Never was stillness here, where I began
To watch alone, to be an emptiness,
To let the strongly running world come in
As seldom can be done: this was to pass
Into no trance but a most brilliant waking,
Active as light upon the deep tide snaking
Before my sight, so lately lost in crowds.
The force that moves all things and lives me out
Made me its filament; all that divides
Time into stints could be no longer thought.

To be had no past tense; all sense was new.
There was no destruction of irrelevance.
A listener to the world, I heard it flow
So huge, so slow, it seemed like permanence
Experienced for an eye-blink. Darting knives
Made slits of light. My years, those forty thieves
Crowded together in one brimming jar,
Let me no wish to grieve for. All this hoard
Was poured out in an instant to the air,
While I was bankrupt even of a word.

Was it some trick to steal the peace of the dead?
This was not peace but power, surely the source
Of every light lit in a transient head

From Genesis to Einstein. In this place
(Austere, coherent, callous), all deeds done,
Bastilles of knowledge, crumpled. The moon's lane,
Quickened with silver, ran; all near was dark;
The land behind most dark. Spread round the sea,
Pinpricks of light timed out a few men's work,
Wakeful in cells impenetrable by me.

Our time seeks for an idol. There is none.
The image that you want is not a city,
Nothing so pitiable; the sea pours in
And shears your dwellings down, ignores your duty
To house a purpose, bears you to extreme.
The lights were warning lights by which I came
As polar travellers come to what is real
In all their banished days. The sight was calm.
There is not any will, or wall, or cell
Would keep this calmness out. Give it no name.

Growing the poem's dumb, planted in change
Immeasurable and ineluctable.
It flowers in light. We reach outside our range
Into the sureness, indestructible,
That sings us out of time. Whose is our voice?
It is the voice of stones that waste, of seas
That cannot rest, of air transfixed by light:
That is to say a human voice, that tries,
Always in solitude, aided by night,
To be identified with all of these.

The sun's white shadow darkened all the sea
With cool and bearable light. I knew this dark:
It was the earth between me and the day
And this my turning place, a boundary mark.
The brittle sea fractured along the coast.
The Irish lights jigged on, fixed points that placed
My world on stone foundations. They put space
A little farther off where men marooned
In granite kept their watch. The moon was glass.
It leaned against a rock, out of the wind.

SYDNEY TREMAYNE

LAZARUS

A simple command cuts his death to the bone.
A stiff shadow, bound, moves out of the cave
Blurred in drifting clouds of recognition.
Dappled with hot shadow of olive-leaves,
Gnarled with the ancient anguish of the vine,
He stood stone-still, carved out of the indrawn
Breath of morning, shriven, his neck arched back
Like a frozen wave. Only the women move,
Mary and Martha rocking to and fro
Like bladderwrack in an indolent undertow.
"Come home from the dead, Lazarus"—
The women had keened away the three nights
Never dreaming their salt and hopeless grief
Could turn their prayer to bitter affirmation.

Over the vibrant silver of the olivetrees,
Across the vine-plants and shadow, the day
Had curled in an arch of lapis lazuli.
Crisp with menace and the dawning voices,
The plumed sunlight coils its force and strikes
A hammer-blow full on the creased eyelids,
On eyeballs wrinkled by the gravebands, bruised
By the brass pennies. Miraculous, the light
Breaks open his eyes as though his skull had split
On some relentless reef of lamentation.
His head strains back, arching his neck to the impact.
The hush of harvest on the taut skins of his ears,
The memorable feel of his own body
Bound still, the animal moanings of the women
Insistent as the fricture of cicadas—
Out of this undertow he claws his way
To a bitter beach of consciousness.

His eyes, unshrouded now, are windows looking
Inward and outward. No eye dare meet them.
Even the women edge their shame away
Disavowing their knowledge and their prayer.

The shrivelled heart may know
The royal reprieve of greenness.
But what imperial purpose,
Infinitely gentle,
Requires this hard penance
Fathering an old crime
On new innocence?

The stiff spasms of his waking overset
The calculus of grief and the cold
Merciful mechanism of forgetting.
His body's musk and myrrh is tropical landfall,
Languid repose transfixed by arrows of regret.
Stricken by the two-edged sword of paradise,
His neck arched back, he raises stone eyes
To the blaze of a bitter vision—pity granting
Life, withholding heaven. Nevertheless
The fluttering hands of embalming sorrow
Quicken like flowers inward, enfold and cherish
A man-child, it may be, or the seeds of a woman's
Grief, or some more numbing, some more precious
Mystery nourished of suffering—perhaps
An alabaster box of spikenard.

For the sword was made flesh
And dwells among us.

George Whalley

MORNING DRAWS NEAR

Morning draws near. Already watery gleams
Seep through, diluting darkness; premonitions
Of dawn run on the air; imminent light
Wells fire along the horizon. Day is waking!
By shore and dune, in meadow, marsh and wood,
To the old torment, to the bloody task
And tragedy of being, to the delight,
The longing and the wonder, life is waking!
Faint pipings prick the dusk, preludes to joy
At the coming of the god; the robin first
With frenzied caroling gives thanks; the wren
The oriole, chewink, flicker and chat
Sound jubilant assent; the thrushes last
With solemn chant antiphonal proclaim
Resurrection and return, spirit is waking!
The spirit that sleeps in metal and in stone,
In flower and tree, in water, earth and air,
And in the spinning demons of the atom,
And in the stars, and in the beast in man
Sleeps, but is growing restless and shall win
A way out of its prison. Hope is waking!
All time present and all time to come,
All time past—the past, which has been the future,
As the future shall be the past—all spirits living,
All spirits that were, all spirits yet to be,
In this brief moment, this eternal now,
Wait on that hope: we are all here together.

JOHN HALL WHEELOCK

III. MUTTERINGS OVER THE CRIB OF A DEAF CHILD

"How will he hear the bell at school
Arrange the broken afternoon,
And know to run across the cool
Grasses where the starlings cry,
Or understand the day is gone?"

Well, someone lifting cautious brows
Will take the measure of the clock.
And he will see the birchen boughs
Outside sagging dark from the sky,
And the shade crawling upon the rock.

"And how will he know to rise at morning?
His mother has other sons to waken,
She has the stove she must build to burning
Before the coals of the night-time die,
And he never stirs when he is shaken."

I take it the air affects the skin,
And you remember, when you were young,
Sometimes you could feel the dawn begin,
And the fire would call you, by and by,
Out of the bed and bring you along.

"Well, good enough. To serve his needs
All kinds of arrangements can be made.
But what will you do if his finger bleeds?
Or a bobwhite whistles invisibly
And flutes like an angel off in the shade?"

He will learn pain. And, as for the bird,
It is always darkening when that comes out.
I will putter as though I had not heard,
And lift him into my arms and sing
Whether he hears my song or not.

JAMES WRIGHT

RITES FOR A DEAD MAGICIAN

(TO HERBERT LINDENBERGER)

Tonight we stand by sea and heap
A holy hill of stone.
The fishes tremble quietly in sleep
Beyond. We form the cairn.

Maybe the lengthened shadow was a ruse
To lure him toward the dark
And drown him: nonetheless we lay our shoes
Aside and sit on rock.

Into his very body folded fire,
The smoky hair shone involute with light;
He quivered with a general desire
By day or night:

Daylight was like a swallow with a splayed
And broken wing. He spelled its parting ghost.
And underneath the wing of night he laid
His hand, and healed whatever wound it had
With ordinary dust.

He saw the mice emerge from balls of grass
To take the morning air;
He leaned above the small innocent face
And whispered in the ear.

Diviningly he scattered running words
Among the sleeping trees,
Called for the otherwise undreaming birds
To waken these
As inner wailings waken to the bards,
And roiling seas.

Do you believe the natural world will bear
To hear a summons thus,
Allow man's tiny lungs to shudder air,
Without the answering curse?

Tonight a swallow plunges down a yawning shade,
A hidden water whines
And claws the petrifaction of the world;
And, knowing these for signs,

I complicate my fingers in the fold
Of rock wherever I can reach,
My hand a starfish feeling in the cold
And eaten beach
To probe the sucking shadow for a hold;
But who will ditch the sea?

And now his body's pale medicinal flower
Feels in the crannied coral, blooming white;
Some of us amble forth to light the pyre,
Spirited stars outrace the slogging night,

Heavy daemonic feet withdraw down air
Behind the burning body on the rock.
Into his very body folds the fire
Of the white moon, into his very hair
The fog is weaving, involute with smoke.

James Wright

LAMENT FOR MY BROTHER ON A HAYRAKE

Cool with the touch of autumn, waters break
Out of the pump at dawn to clear my eyes;
I leave the house, to face the sacrifice
Of hay, the drag and death. By day, by moon,
I have seen my younger brother wipe his face
And heave his arm on steel. He need not pass
Under the blade to waste his life and break;

The hunching of the body is enough
To violate his bones. That bright machine
Strips the revolving earth of more than grass;
Powered by the fire of summer, bundles fall
Folded to die beside a burlap shroud;
And so my broken brother may lie mown
Out of the wasted fallows, winds return,
Corn-yellow tassels of his hair blow down,
The summer bear him sideways in a bale
Of darkness to October's mow of cloud.

JAMES WRIGHT

UNDERGRADUATE POETRY

SONGS OF A SPEARMAN

. . . THE SEA IS LIKE A LOVER . . .

I lie along the waters,
where the sunlight is a sea-thing,
a captive in the moving mesh of light
that sifts down and down
to where life rocks
with the deepest rhythms of the ocean.
I move with liquid movements
there, among the fish, and brush
the outstretched branchings
of the weeds that wave in the waves
that gave them life.
The embracing element,
in the mould of my body!
These profound currents that move
the fish and the weeds move me,
and caress me,
and it seems that I am a sea-thing, too,
and the sea is like a lover loving me.

. . . WHERE FIRST THINGS BREATHED . . .

Let me lie with the ocean,
and have my heart-beat beating
with the pulse of passing waves;
let the ocean enfold me,
and hold me completely,
lie under me, above,
and along all my sides.
Then—remembering the time
when Time began, and the world
was still on fire—
let me pillow my head
on those passing waves,
and whisper words
more deep than desire:
"Look—at last I've returned!"

GRAEME WICKS

"RISING UP NOTE . . ."

Rising up note upon note, the magnificat
Gains the arched roof of my sorrow,
Over the top it flies, outstripping the ego.
I wonder, kneeling there, wonder in mystery.
The carved wood, the brass, the cross.
Coloured glass and grey light, shadows,
Voices, those voices chanting now the Lord's Prayer,
Flowers stretching out in the darkness,
    "Wetting the silken borders of her veil . . ."
I cry to you against the solid backs of churchgoers
Adamant in their tweed and fur:
    Pray for me, pray for me,
Toss those voices into the shadows
High in the roof, with Alleluias
Rebounding like bright, coloured balls
On a flashing fountain in the sun.
There they go, off into the air, above our heads,
I cannot reach them, they never fall
Into my outstretched hands,
But ever toss higher,
The blue, the red, the gold . . .
Bursting stars flaring around us
For me they join the black air,
The singing dies softly, the candles snuffed,
File out, the service is over this day.
But inside the singing goes on
Bounding against the roof of my soul,
As I feel the night air cool about me
And vainly reach out to catch at the sound.

April Pemberton

PRAISE OF WASTELANDS

Here on a desert at night where driftwood
Or wormwood has bleached all day on the sand
Where children never wander hand in hand,
The leper who has lost his bell and hood
Lives, prays and counts the stars.

Here, answer to a thousand lost afars,
The end of this world waits in place not time
To hold him in peace whose bondage is done,
To shelter in rock-cleft solitude one
Who found no reason when he scanned the rhyme.

Here in the drifting dunes the hermit sees
Tomorrow turn to sand to meet today,
Yet smiles because what's dust cannot decay;
And tells upon spilt stone-bead rosaries
The time turned world of lives that stop and start.

Here sharpness is not used to cut the heart.
It only serves to clarify, to clear.
Sand gives no promise like wavering grain:
Here one is cloistered from joy and its pain.
Here in the shade rock; here in the sand. Here.

MARGARET LAMB

WAIT AND MOVE WITH ME

Wait and move with me
Under the sun-starred sea
To crash in among the drenched rocks,
To sink a lifetime deep
Among them, these stones of
Colored world-light. Deeper,
Deeper than the lifetime
Of a grain of sand to sink
In that unwearying knowledge
Of the birth below.

For the gulls are flying in
To shore, out of the sea's womb,
Heralding the genesis in
The rising sun. Oh wait,
Rest in the moment of an early shadow,
And hand in hand we will dive
Among the unborn children
Of the fruitful searocks,
And rise, seaweed-strung,
With a springtime tale,
Praise of sun-bearing joy to heaven.

PETER FISH

CHIAROSCURO

> ". . . for how we live is so far removed from how we ought to live, that he who abandons what is done for what ought to be done, will rather bring about his own ruin than his preservation."
>
> —MACHIAVELLI

I, Thales, carpenter and financier
when to be rich was to be busy,
plied Egyptian mathematics for a way
of estimating distances at sea. Miletus in our day
was no luxurious Phaeacia, kept no bards and beggars . . .
Where Mycenaean houses reared
high ceilings, I built second floors,
and advocated comfortable chairs
in place of heavy, awkward thrones. My pains
were well rewarded; with perfected
instruments, our argosies pursued
a certain course, our crops no longer
feared astrology.
And in the trivial leisure
of my old age, I composed
a plausible cosmology of "elements" to satisfy
the superstitious of the old-world—substituting
modest pantheism for idolatry, plain observation
for surmise. For what I see and hear
and sensibly deduce, I stand on. Not philosophy,
but craft made possible the pyramids.

This week the pastures offer flowers
in profusion . . . and today we crucified
a madman, who offended us with grand
pretensions to divinity. In the muddy streets
the children jeered at him affecting
martyrdom; it was Jerusalem's spring-cleaning
of unwanted ideologies . . .

One afternoon,
across the barren Campo de Monteil
a gangling sad man rode, on a broken-down
plough-horse. Armed against the mediocrity
of "what is," shrining in his old man's heart
"what ought to be," he tilts with magic knights
in castles of the wandering mind.
Though mournful from bad fortune and misunderstanding,
since he bore a lance and wore full armour,
death, when it came, was natural. His *apologia*
might read: "He knew himself, and not the world."

ARTHUR FREEMAN

THE COMING OF AUTUMN

Autumn is time of fall and time of breaking;
Our independent colours burn from green
And in late valleys the last fruits are taken

From nerveless boughs; the ranks of pickers leave
These cold trees to a winter's lonely shaking.
Wet roads drive on and interlock and weave

Past fallen leaves which mark the time of burning
Come round again. And, as the tree will grieve
Waking into a naked April morning

To learn the full significance of loss,
The family finds one heart no more returning
And bears departure like a bitter cross

Which he, far off, no longer feels, awaking
To new fruition. The parents turn and toss
With fire at their hearts. But fallen leaves are dross;
Autumn is time of breaking and of burning.

CHRIS WALLACE-GRABBE

HIDDEN SUMMER

". . . February flies, with little summers
Hidden in its beard: unlicensed mummers
Performing April antics for a day."

MARK VAN DOREN, *A Winter Diary*

The snow has crept away, leaving the ground
Mucky under tattered leaves.
A snowman slumps, perspiring into the earth
As if his melting self
Hurried on to catch the mauve-white mass
That left him behind.

The hills hang out a friendly
Brownish-yellow sign: At Home.
Along the twisted road lie bulbous walnuts
That drank too much.
Heavily they rest like fat, black toads,
Too full to hop away.

White-green sprouts popped through the ground
last night;
The moisture sucked them up.
Timorously they hide beneath dank weeds
And bits of bark.
Hot sun will strengthen later plants, but these,
Like pallid moths, die soon.

Rambunctious, awkward, elfin wind pushes, puffs
and teases;
Promising facetiously
An early warmth, the fiendish imp, at gullibles
Blows frostily and swirls away
To wrinkle sterling-silver lakes and crackle
Islands floating there.

Yesterday beyond the hills some mountains, lately
hidden,
Stretched into their places.

Motionless they waited, cued
For the rising of the fog.
They face the glinting yellow "spot"
In character, tableaued.

The path over the hill to the boathouse road
Holds a kindergarten of rain droplets
That spent the morning making slush pies. Grown-up
raindrops
Mixed the slush:
They stopped and splashed and beat until
The snow's insides were all squashed out.

In twilight gusts the evening wind, worn out and
irritated,
Coldly hurries darkened clouds
Across the skies to darken hills where shivering walnuts
Roll away and straining sprouts
Bend down to find their holes but cannot . . .
Winter threatens everything.

One man shuts both eyes
Against the passing scenes. He dreams
Of the slower trip
Behind him. He walks in thought
Through memory prints, mirages
In pink, green, ivory.

Another stares ahead
Into the translucent steam rising at the whistle.
This man arrives most quickly
At the end of the journey; he has paid no attention
To the past or the present
And one day whizzes into Oblivion.

The time of man's life passes
Each day faster. Its momentum increases
Like that of a little streamliner.
Life glides its passengers with round-trip tickets
Into a journey away from and circling to
Eternity.

NANCY GODWIN

BEGAN ON THE JAMES

Can you show me where the river ends
and I began?
The river is the dark blood; slow and languid
in my Southern veins.
The river is the white spume of my courage
flaunting itself on boulders
mute and immovable.
The river is clay and dust and moonlight,
bearing a sprig of lilac down the rapids,
rocking a broken barge where the wharf has fallen.
It lingers at Richmond, loving the templed slope,
tasting the mellowed is and was that yet shall be.
We are the same, the River James and I.
Look for us now, curved against mountains,
tomorrow part of the pulse that throbs into the sea.

ALIX ARLENE INGHAM

VILLANELLE OF THE DYING YEAR

The dying year goes out in rain and cold,
Shadow of winter overhangs the time,
And in this death men find their deaths foretold.

A violent end: The passing-bell is tolled
For a poet killed on the roads, who had some fame;
The dying year goes out in rain and cold.

May we not die before we've time to mould
Some perfect thing in bronze, or intricate rhyme,
Where men may find their deaths and glories told.

And may our faltering resolution hold
Though a poet die still young and the wind scream;
The dying year goes out in rain and cold.

May our achievement comfort us when old,
And hearten those who come the way we came,
That they may find a peaceful death foretold.

O Child, we bring You incense, myrrh and gold,
Dwell in our storm, O Peace and living Flame;
The dying year goes out in rain and cold,
And in this death men find their deaths foretold.

PHILIP MARTIN

THIS LOVE

For lack of resolution, I remembered.
And down desire and the hand's track,
From the speech of warm tongues,
I brought her back.

Abandoned in the dreaming search for islands,
I summoned her there,
The moist seal of her palm,
The charm of the spice of her hair.

In the cool margins of the night
I drew her fair,
But our love was an ark of fragile animals,
Nothing shaped of air.

Memory reflects like a tear,
Distorting my face within her eye,
And these memories I built
Leached the ashes for the lie.

This love is a commentary on our time,
Where sweet lust is a grope
And preys with the false heart's easy rhetoric
Upon the bone and flesh of hope.

Instead of this taxidermy of the spirit
I would have been young as fire,
To restore to ruling lips
The metaphysics of desire.

ROBERT REHDER

VALEDICTION

After the slow sad hours of night,
The rose-unfolding hours of night,
That hid the desert and the tilth alike,
The ashen city lit with guns,
The small mysterious English fields,
Chilled by a silver-salver moon;

Before the first thin scissor slits of light,
The flower-opening, eyelid-opening light
That paled the fires, the stars alike,
And stilled the spurting guns,
When beasts were stirring in the English fields
And swans winged westward with the moon;

Just as the lace of branches came in sight,
The deep-browed tall-stacked manor came in sight,
Its woodcock brick, its lawns alike,
And men could see the havoc of the guns,
And beasts could see the mist scarves on the fields,
And stars grew pale and eyeless as the moon;

One brother woke in his familiar room and felt afraid,
Yet knew not why.
The other, waking in the blood and rubble, said
"I do not fear to die."

JOHN VILLIERS

LOVE SONG

The bud is beginning to break on the tree,
The voice of the turtle is heard in the land,
The promise of blossom will quicken in me

To the cry of a bird, and the fledgling will be
My love and my dove whom the Canticles band
When the bud is beginning to break on the tree.

Make haste my beloved, arise, you will see
How the shoot of my love pushes forth and has
    planned
This promise of blossom that quickens in me.

My beloved came leaping the mountains; now we
Skip over the hills, and the hills understand
That the bud is beginning to break on the tree,

For winter is past. Now the hart running free
In his love, will return. So sweetly I stand
With the promise of blossom that quickens in me,

The flower of the valley, the lilies that he
Will desire, and gather with tenderest hand
When the buds are beginning to break on the tree,
In promise of blossom that quickens in me.

DOLORES WARWICK